Don't Be Selfish, Share Your Art With the World

Copyright © 2017 by Emmett Ferguson

All rights reserved. No portion of this book may be reproduced, stored in a retrieval system, or transmitted in any form or by any means-electronic, mechanical, photocopy, recording, scanning or other-except for brief quotations in critical reviews or articles, without the prior written permission from the Publisher.

Published by Magistri Entertainment, LLC

ISBN-13: 978-1977854520 | **ISBN-10:** 1977854524

This book has opinions and ideas of the author. It is intended to give helpful and informative material on the subjects addressed in the publication. It is sold with the understanding that the author – and publisher are not engaged in giving professional tax and or legal advice or any other kind of personal or professional services in the book.

The reader should consult his or her consultants, tax and financial advisor, attorney or other competent professional before adopting any of the concepts in this book or drawing inferences from it. The content of this book, by its very nature, is general. Meanwhile, each reader's situation is unique. Therefore, as with all books of this nature, the purpose is to give general information rather than address individual situations, which books by their very nature cannot do.

The author and publisher specifically disclaim all responsibility for any liability, loss, or risk, personal or otherwise, which is incurred consequently, directly or indirectly, of the use and application of any of the contents of this book.

*Inspired by all the artists, entrepreneurs,
and influencers who share their stories every day.*

Contents

Foreword by Paul Kanter...1

Introduction..7

1. Don't Be Selfish..10
2. Always Learn..17
3. Leadership and Artists..29
4. Increase Your Network...37
5. Impact the World..46
6. Opportunity in Social Media..56
7. Plan Your Artistic Future...66
8. Share Your Value with the World..76
9. Monetize...83
10. Fearlessly Pursue Your Work..89

Foreword

By Paul Kanter

"There is always a way. Don't be afraid of something you don't understand or any obstacles that fall in the way, take a deep breath and pick up a resource to learn to overcome those hindrances. Absolute gratification comes when you achieve both your big and small goals."

- William Gant, Escape Room Entrepreneur

When learning a new skill, you find that every teacher has their own unique style. Ten different artists will teach the same material in ten different ways, and you find one or two of them whose style resonates with you more than the others. This applies to every aspect of the art making process. It is easy then to get lost in information, to be inspired by established artists but have lingering doubts about your own art, your own vision and goals. There are books and online resources that focus on art techniques, others on the business side of art, and much more rarely focus on the spiritual and creative side of art; the creative side that nourishes the soul, inspires and motivates, brings happiness to and has a positive impact in the lives of others.

This is more than just a how-to book, it's more than a motivational book that you can turn to when in need of motivation, although it succeeds as being that. This volume also presents a unique and compelling vision of art making that connects every aspect of an artist's life to the larger life of humanity and of the planet, to a unifying process of sharing and giving that is rooted in our common humanity. Whenever you are lost for some guidance regarding your work, or if you are questioning your work's value, or your own, or are wondering if you can make a difference in people's lives with your art, here is your guide and the answers to those questions.

The message contained in this book focuses on every aspect of the creative process, but always with an emphasis on the spiritual and creative nature of the artist and their audience, their humanity, their dreams and aspirations.

If you as an artist have ideas and a vision for the art you want to make, have devoted time and energy to learning techniques and the fundamentals of the craft, but are hampered or stressed by doubts, negative thinking, or the negativity we often experience in society, this book will inspire and motivate you on every page. It will unlock your spirit from negativity and doubts and have you thinking in new ways so that nothing blocks you from sharing the beauty and creativity you wish to share with the world.

In the larger conversation around work-life balance, of finding meaning in work and in life, and of ways in which people and communities can find meaning and can work together to solve problems, Emmett adds the role the arts can play. This book will motivate you to maintain your own creative and spiritual balance in your life as you create the art that moves you most, connect with others in life, and realize your higher spiritual goals.

Emmett has always been about helping others. In so doing, he has connected audiences with inspiring independent filmmakers and their art. This book is a natural extension of that work.

I myself am lucky to be able to call Emmett a mentor and a friend. Emmett has a gift for unlocking the hidden potential and passion within artists and inspiring them to share their visions with a world that needs and desires such creative visions. He understands the larger impact that the arts can have on people's lives as well as artists' own desires to create works that inspires the public.

He reminds us of our desires for community, happiness, and a healthy and beautiful world. If whenever you feel doubt in your life or are unsure of yourself, this book is here to remind you of the amazing gifts that you have and how you can right now share those gifts with the world.

It doesn't just talk about the tools for making and sharing your art, it inspires the soul and spirit to give to the world and to connect with the world. Emmett does everything he can to encourage you at every step of the way. More than that, he sets up a unique paradigm for looking at your art practice.

Emmett and I shot a project for a fun festival for independent filmmakers. The festival gives teams of small independent teams the limitation of writings, shooting, and completing a film in just two days over a weekend. I was in a play-reading group with Emmett, and he asked me if I would like to be the director for his team. I was ecstatic, as filmmaking was a passion of mine, but I never had the confidence to create a team to make a film.

Over the course of the weekend, I worked with a team of actors and friends of Emmett who helped as crew. We worked tirelessly through the weekend, shooting the film and editing it and adding a soundtrack, burning it to DVD. For me, there was nothing like the feeling of accomplishment a we rushed down the streets of Fort Lauderdale, FL, like the last sprint to the finish line, to the bar the festival was using as its drop-off point for team's finished films. We handed in our film, which was later shown at a screening of all the team's films.

The experience taught both of us a lot. He as a producer and me as director. My experience as an independent director, I also knew that if you yourself wanted anything to be in the film, it was your responsibility to make that happen. If you didn't do it, and take responsibility for your vision of the film, those props, ideas, or scenes, would not be in the finished film. That weekend we worked with amazing local actors and even newcomers who had the opportunity to shine in their first film roles. It would not be their last film roles.

This book has a unique message: You have a gift for art. Give your art to the world. Your art has value. This idea permeates this book. From discussing the value of the art and artists of the past, to the value your art can have for others. By covering everything to creating your art to sharing and selling your art to others, Emmett's vision of art and the value of each artist is a clear and enlightening vision of the positive impact and beauty art gives to the world. That positivity and beauty becomes a goal for the artist, positivity and beauty as the artist sees it, and because of that, it manifests itself in the moment in which the art is created.

The unique potential of an artist is surveyed from their inner vision and ideas to their outer goals and means of sharing their unique vision with others. The short length of this volume makes it readable in an afternoon or an evening, with time to spare to put its ideas into action the very same day.

By explaining how artists can share or sell their art, and encouraging them to do so, Emmett shares a mindset that continually strives to give something of value. Manifested in an artist' work from the very beginning of the creative process is this focus on giving something of value, something that makes a difference in people's lives.

Introduction

"We're all born with natural talents. For some of us, it's clear from the start what we're great at. For others, it takes a while to discover it."

– Michael Riley, Writer and Blogger

If a person never lets the world know about the artist within, have they truly lived? There is more to you than meets the eye. There is a story in you that no one else can tell. You have a view of the world no one else has, a voice that can change the way people see, live, taste, breathe, and more. Do not let yourself go unexpressed, unshared, undiscovered.

This is not a self-help, hand-holding book meant to guide you through life to become a happier person. This book is a call to action to create art and share it with the world. This book is a reminder to not allow your creativity to go to waste.

If you have never done any art, or have a few sketches on sticky notes at your place of work and want to do more, let this book motivate you to expand. If you are currently pursuing art, or do art as a hobby, let this book drive you to get your work out to the world instead of keeping it hidden. If you are already a successful artist, allow this book to motivate you to work on a bigger project, help more people, and inspire change to improve the world. We are all at different levels, but we are always capable of more.

Do not have a fear of pursuing right-brained activities, but most of all, prepare yourself mentally by eliminating your fear of having others recognize your work. Whether you want to pursue work as a painter or entertainer or creative, you must learn the tools to present your creativity. This book discusses the opportunities available to create a larger impact. We discuss the individual skills necessary to share your work. You must take it upon yourself to get started and take the initiative to put in the work to have people know.

By the end of this book, you should expect to complete at least your first masterpiece. Everyone has made a doodle or written a story as a school activity, but has everyone honestly attempted to pursue art as a hobby or career? It is viable if you truly desire and aim to do it. Whether you need to combine multiple skills, practice first as a hobby, or get inspiration first, know that you have everything you need within. You just have to do it.

1. Don't Be Selfish

"I feel it's our responsibility to share the importance of our vision as artists to help shape and inspire others to continue to create and make their dreams into reality."

– Stacy Newton, Author

There are greater opportunities to inspire others than ever before. By keeping your art, your creativity, and your voice to yourself, you are being selfish. There are more than seven billion people in the world today, many of whom value what you create. They might even be waiting for it. Become an artist, be a voice for others, and inspire others. Share your perspective of the world. How the sky looks, how your steak dinner looks, what your last date looked like and more. Share your vision.

Art comes in many forms including painting, sculpting, writing, turning trash into treasure, and even building businesses are considered an art form. There is even art in cooking steaks and making sales. You do not have to define what your art is now, but it is important to begin your search, experiment, and share. Art is an exciting medium that allows exploration of undiscovered worlds, answers to impossible questions, and creates meaning where it is needed.

Friends, family, and people you might not even know yet are waiting for something to call them to action. Others are seeking inspiration, motivation, a reason to keep doing what they are doing. People are finding answers, and you might just have the enlightenment they're looking for.

By creating and sharing art, you are creating opportunities for others to learn from you. You are bringing value to the world. You can also use your art, your voice to support other causes you believe in.

Everyone on the planet is now more connected than ever. You can take a picture of your painting, share a film, and deliver a book to hundreds of thousands of people and more at the click of a button. Now, you will need to put in work, and you cannot expect overnight success, but the opportunity is out there because of our technology today.

Social media allows you to connect with CEO's, celebrities, and global leaders at the click of a button. Word of mouth gets around faster than ever because of the internet. With digital e-commerce platforms, you can even sell your work to support your goals to create even more.

Improvements in technology allow you to share your ideas faster than ever. It also allows those who share common interests to find your work faster than ever. Historically, artists left their creativity in dusty books, dark caverns, on walls, in temples, and many forgotten places.

As romantic as it is to imagine your work being uncovered centuries from now and regarded highly, let's ask "where is the work of Michelangelo, Picasso, Van Gogh, Matisse, Beethoven, and Mozart today?" They can all be found online anyway. Do not let romanticism allow you to be forgotten or lost. Let the idea of becoming great, while you are alive drive you to continue sharing your work. Take a chance and sell your creation, because if you don't, someone else might.

Your art can do more than just be "looked at" or "analyzed. Become an artrepeneur. Let your art be a way for you to not only share your unique perspective but bring value to more lives. By starting a business around your art, you can give back to non-profit organizations.

If you reach higher levels of success, you can help pay others to work for you as they continue finding theirs. Nothing significant can is accomplished alone. The greatest painters and writers in history may have created their works by themselves, but they had inspiration from others whether it be a romantic relationship, a unique childhood, or a chance meeting with a stranger. Artists create plays for actors, sonatas for pianists, and even comic books for production companies.

Let your creative potential soar, but more than that, share it. All you need to do is start doing. There is no reason to continue letting that doodle stay in your pen, or that idea for an op-ed article get forgotten in your mind. Let a friend read it. Let your dog smell the art in confusion, and make a video of it. Leave it in a park for others to see. Share it and begin connecting with others who share your interest.

The world needs great leaders. Leaders can come in all different forms: silent, loud, aggressive, laid-back, detail-oriented, innovative, efficient, and more. Artists lead and inspire too. Do not waste your voice and the power you have, to create and help others.

Consider for a moment the renaissance, the baroque era, and even the nineties (that's nineteen-nineties). Art has had an impact in every period of human existence. There is a reason we no longer wear leaf skirts or bell bottoms in most cases. It is because of creative artists envisioning a change in the way we dress. There are also historical reminders through art about what the past was like, and how our ancestors communicated. Perhaps your creations may create positive social movements. Art survives.

You might not create a bestseller with your first book, painting, play, or business. The only way to fail is never to try or never share. What you consider an ugly piece of work might be prime for a gallery appearance of ugly works. There are even people who enjoy the process of creating a masterpiece. Ever visit a museum and gain inspiration by the unfinished doodles of renowned artists? Let yourself experiment, feel what works, feel what is right. Then share it and go after your next idea.

You might feel accomplished with one piece, but why let it stop you? Surely you have more to share with the world. Why keep it to yourself? Make something new, for yourself, and for others.

Continue honing your skills, and by learning the rules, or the right way of doing something, you will know which ones to break and be considered an artistic genius. Continue developing your bodies of work and search for more reasons to create, more messages you want to share, and more ways for you to inspire, even if it's just you.

Experiment with the means to improve your work, but also ways to sell and share your work. Keeping it to yourself will not sustain your efforts. Where will you get motivation? Intrinsic motivation is excellent, but it does not help others. Keep repeating. Repeating makes practice, and practice makes perfect. That is probably in a book somewhere. Keep creating and moving people.

Let art represent the best and worst of you. Share the lowest moments and the highest moments. Most importantly, be yourself, and do not hold back. There may be opportunities to reprint a piece of work for distribution, but there is a uniqueness to you that no one can copy better. There are millions of people too scared to share their story with the world. There is so much to be said, including yours. Inspire others.

Consider leaving your work for others to remember you by. Perhaps they may not own one of your works, but they may have seen it, inspiring them to do something great down the road. What will you be remembered by? An heirloom? A business? A book? A painting? An inspiring word? Leave your creativity for others where they can find it: not hidden in a cellar. Someone will value what you share. Do not be afraid to sell and share it.

Do not let fear make you selfish. Do not let another person's selfishness and insecurity hinder your progress. By sharing your work, you have an opportunity to connect with many more like-minded creatives who can help support your endeavor. Do not let petty criticisms be an obstacle to your potential as an artist. With your work, you have a voice. Let that be a vehicle to help those who feel helpless, find theirs.

2. Always Learn

"No matter who you are, creating something from nothing is a daunting task. The fear that you might fail is always present. But my greatest satisfaction and biggest successes in life have come from forcing myself to overcome resistance, and push past fear to see what was possible."

— Trevor O. Munson, Screenwriter

If you are an expert in your field, this chapter can help you explore new mediums of expression. There are many ways to learn skills or knowledge: by sound, by sight, and hands on. Regardless of how you learn, you must start doing now. I've left a small blank space purposely for you to do something, anything. Write a sentence in your next book, draw a doodle, write one business idea. If you are more advanced and already have a portfolio, take a moment to write your next project or draw a doodle that takes you to the next level. Share it with me.

***

***

Use the space above as an opportunity to start your portfolio. It does not have to be perfect, but start getting your technique down no matter how small you think the task is.

Continue building your skills and confidence. When you have confidence in your work and yourself, you will be happier, but also find opportunities to create more and better work. Do not get overconfident, but believe in the fact that your art is the start of something larger than yourself.

There are plenty of techniques that help build confidence like improving posture or reading books. Gaining confidence will also prepare you to begin promoting your art to the world and grow as an artist. Remember, we want to be an unselfish artist because we can share our creativity to help others.

It is also time to learn good habits and unlearn bad habits. Think of some of the bad habits you have: procrastination, self-defeating notions, and other negative thoughts. Write them down, throw them away and end them. Find the opposing healthy habits and begin doing those instead. This will continue to help you build the confidence to start doing and sharing.

Remember, find good practices. There are plenty of resources and methods to help you develop better habits and mentalities. Take a moment to research those if this is where you struggle before pursuing your art.

Sometimes you get stuck. You run out of ideas. You get writer's block. You get stuck on a problem and cannot figure out how to fix it. Use this time to find inspiration; even if its' from a past work that you can look at and improve. Maybe you just need time away from the project to clear your mind and meditate. Research has shown meditation helps the brain. There is also an endless amount of inspiration past and present online. Watch videos, read articles, find free classes. Do not let a self-inflicted thought obstacle stop you from moving forward with something you love.

Take a moment to find your nearest museum. Many are free, low cost, or have free days. You can visit a library and read art books, or research galleries online. This is a chance for you to be some of the most artistic and creative minds the world has come to admire. Do not just walk through the museum. Take moments, to stop and absorb what artists are saying. It is challenging to do this with your own work, and that is not your fault, which is why it is a great chance to examine and think about others works. You might find the answers to your questions.

Per an internet search I did, there were nearly One Hundred and Thirty Million books published. There might be more by the time you look it up. I expect you to add one to that list. While not all books are relevant to you, there are secrets in many books including answers to your questions. You know what is great about libraries? You have hundreds of books on all sorts of topics. It is a wonderful opportunity to learn about other people, expand your horizons, and improve your ability to connect with people from all different backgrounds. You can take a broad approach at finding books, or you can focus in on one subject at a time and learn even more about it. Learn about paintings, businesses, and musicians throughout history.

There are many types of books you can read. As an artist, you have an opportunity to learn from the greatest artists of all time, through their biographies. Learn the stories of success and understand the fact that there is no such thing as overnight success. Hear about the challenges others faced and how they are like the ones you face right now.

If you are brand new and have no clue where to start, a biography might give you inspiration for something to imitate. Now, in the future, you want to be yourself, but to start, if you need to emulate a good habit such as writing five-thousand words per day that some author practiced, then do so. Do not plagiarize.

Practice becoming better by understanding how successful people become better. You also have an opportunity to learn from others' attempts and not follow that path, or even try to succeed where others have not.

Concerning creating good habits, you can begin by setting goals. I left the space below for you to write down one goal. This can be any goal big or small. Perhaps you want to write five stories by the end of the year. As you work towards that goal (or not), you can multiply it and adjust it. But do something, here is your space:

***

***

You now have something to work toward. Whatever you wrote down, you have an opportunity to multiply it. Take this next moment to enhance the goal. Take your goal and raise it higher. Did you want to write five stories? Double that! Triple it! Did you want to start a cancer research company? Enlarge your goals even higher! Add and consider your own list of diseases and global issues you want to cure.

Do not just launch a cancer research company, start a business that will cure cancer and other diseases. Find the art you want to share with the world. Let this goal setting be a way to push yourself, and be your own boss.

How do we work towards those incredible goals we have set for ourselves that we just multiplied or escalated? Create a reward system for yourself at certain milestones. Want to find a cancer cure? Find a way to reward yourself if you read five books about cancer. Or reward yourself after you have spoken with five or ten scientists about cancer. Or reward yourself after you have volunteered for 40 hours at a cancer research facility.

Many rewards may be intrinsic, but the idea here is to set small milestones to reach as you work towards the goal. And do not worry, these can change. You should expect change, but simplify your greatest ambitions into small and large steps.

As we begin exploring all the opportunities to build creativity and start doing and creating our art, we must also develop senses and absorb other works better. Do not just visit a museum and walk through. Force yourself to stop at each painting you see, and time yourself to look at each painting for at least two minutes or five minutes even. Write an entire page of your journal on just one painting no matter how long it takes.

Sit and think deeply about a subject or work. Enjoy it. If it is music, try to feel it and absorb the lyrics, notes, and emotion it is trying to elicit. Begin to absorb creativity and art. Eventually, you can release what you have absorbed in your own form.

If you have not already started doing so, you will need to gather materials. Sometimes all you need is a pencil, pen, and paper. Other times you need inspiration. We should know where inspiration is by now. But let's decide on an art form and gather the materials. Piano too expensive? There are tools online that let you play and experiment with keys by clicking. Go to a local music store and touch and feel those instruments. Is a camera too expensive? Use your phone, borrow from some friends, ask for money to buy a super cheap camera.

There are plenty of non-profit resources that support the arts, and if you look hard enough, you can find a way to express yourself, share your voice, and create art. There is no excuse to not create at this very moment.

It is important to remember testing is a part of the process. Scientists do experiments. Artists doodle, write drafts and brainstorm. Entrepreneurs test businesses. Inventors tinker. Every success requires trying new things and testing.

Begin by coming up with ideas of what you want to create then take small steps. Do not be scared to restart. Destruction from volcanoes has been known to create new life on islands. By testing yourself and trying new art, you can also uncover what you do not understand, and figure out where you need to focus your development.

We are in an incredibly connected time, but here is also where it gets challenging. If your primary art is not technology based (digital editing, building websites, architectural drafting), then you will need to begin learning technology. You can explore the idea of selling on e-commerce platforms, building simple websites, and exploring online groups with similar passions.

We have so far discussed diving in and finding inspiration and doing. Now is where we must find opportunities to share our work. Skills can be as simple as taking a photo of our grilled hamburger masterpiece and uploading it. Now, at the time of writing this book, I would say most the world knows how to use simple tools.

There are plenty of resources for you to begin learning how to leverage the internet to succeed, and we will discuss them briefly in later chapters, but not now. Just start thinking of technology (mostly web platforms) to share, market, and sell.

Through the internet or face to face networking, as artists, we must market ourselves. If your goal in life is to create art only for yourself and never share it, and never have it discovered, that is fair too. But for the artist who wants to bring tremendous value to the world, they must market themselves or find others to market for them.

This is more than just relentless self-promotion. This is sharing your own story and the story of your work to inspire others to create. Marketing is about finding how your work fits into others' lives and how it helps. Learn to network and learn to share and learn to market. Marketing itself is an art form and so is selling.

After people begin learning about your art and the value it brings, you must sell. This is a way to sustain yourself. Selling also helps build self-confidence. You can sell your work through e-commerce platforms or traditional galleries. You can sell your work on the streets of your nearest city. You have worked hard to hone your craft, create, restart, and master.

If your work can make someone's apartment look nicer, then they should have the opportunity to buy it. Do not just tell other people about how awesome your art is. Let them have a piece of it for themselves.

The amount of learning to create and share great valuable art may seem overwhelming. Creating is not easy, marketing is not easy, and selling is not easy. Nothing great is easy. However, this is not a single step process. As you take each step on your journey, you will find new passions, scrap old projects, focus on strengths, and find others to help you with your weaknesses.

Your mind will begin tying concepts together. Every new learning opportunity creates an idea for you to work with. But do not let your art float around only to be forgotten.

3. Leadership and Artists

"Don't expect anyone to fill your bowl for you. You must fill it yourself, over and over and over and over."

– Sarah London, Filmmaker and Photographer

Education improves society through advancements in science, technology, engineering, and mathematics. Meanwhile, art drives social change, inspires great messages, provides historical insight, and leaves traces of our present day. As education helps us live longer, healthier, and more prosperous lives, art gives voice and fulfills us mentally providing a way to share our unique thoughts with the world.

Creating art is not just a way to share unique perspectives, but it is also a way to inspire and grow others. While some find comfort studying mathematical algorithms, others are more suited to find undiscovered beauty. Create art and lead others to see the world differently.

The ancient Egyptians developed hieroglyphs to communicate. Architects design skyscrapers to house people in buildings that look aesthetically appealing in the skyline. Writers share untold stories, musicians entertain us with soothing sounds, and painters create images that make us wonder. Do not create thinking your art has no value.

The art you create will have an impact, and it could have a profound effect on others. Attach your art to a message, something you want to tell the world, even if it is about your significant other. Fill a void on someone's wall or in a toy box. Lead by creating valuable art.

The greatest artists in the world were part of some movement. They changed perspectives, they were great orators, and they combined their education to invent new solutions to the world's problems. Be an artist, and through your creativity, become a leader. Begin to share your work and as people recognize your work, find ways to bring more value.

Many people struggle to find their voice. They spend most of their lives trying to figure out a way to express themselves and speak out against injustices or share their unique views of the world. Your voice can be lost as time forgets you, or you can influence others with your art. You can share your art in galleries and with other influential figures to get your message across. Use your art to generate awareness for important causes such as ending hunger. You also do not always have to "save the world." You can develop your unique method of creating art that others may follow and gain inspiration from.

If you live in a place with the freedom and luxury to pursue art (unrestricted) as more than a hobby, you are incredibly fortunate. Whether you create a more visually appealing world or write a book no one can ignore, there is a chance for a better world. Tying to social change that moves you, whether it is a change in taste of music or a satire about current political issues can help you focus your work as well. Think about ways to generate awareness about an issue, person, or event. Even if your message does not instantly appeal to massive audiences, keep trying and do not give up.

It is rare if not impossible for anyone to come up with something that has never been done before. Every creation originates from some idea or thought that is already in existence, or has existed at some point in history. If someone comes up with a way to travel through time, it probably stems from the foundational research of highly esteemed scientists.

When others see people like them developing their voice, they will follow. They will find hope and try to create art too. Empowering others to share their stories and find their success is a social activity. So is painting, playing music, acting, and building a business.

It is necessary to market and sell your art, but also important is sharing your story. Give others the opportunity to learn from your success or mistakes. Scientists heavily document their procedures as they try to save the world. By sharing your own story, you can begin to relate more to those around you. As you focus down on who you are, you can then begin to create art that speaks to you more. When your art speaks to you, you can find those who may appreciate your art as well.

As you share your story of artistic success, people will want to copy, share, and even steal your work and ideas to develop their unique voice. Do not let this frighten you. The more you succeed, the more you have an opportunity to help others. Eventually, your word can contribute to creating opportunities for other budding artists, or be enough to save a life.

As you become a more successful artist generating awareness, other artists and leaders have an opportunity to recognize you as well. When people begin to pursue art, they connect with other like-minded people, and as they get better, they connect with even more successful likeminded people.

Share your work in local galleries, at the local pub, through Instagram, or even just on the side of a building. If you have not quite yet developed your own body of work, you can begin by curating others works and learn from them. As you come to master your technique, find opportunities to discuss the methods of those who you consider experts.

Figure out what inspires you and begin to seek out opportunities to combine others works with your own personal perspectives. Share both your story, your learnings, and more. It is not necessary to share every detail because some attitudes are tough to describe, but to share what you learn, is to help others grow. You are only as successful as those you help.

Do not make an exact copy of another's work except perhaps in private to learn some technique such as a brush stroke or visually pleasing design. Find opportunities to meld your ideas with the ideas of your biggest inspirations, only then, can you become great. As you begin building greater success, others will bounce ideas off you without you knowing.

Do not get intimidated by other's success, continue honing your craft and take solace in the idea that you are inspiring others. Real talented artists will create based off what they learn from you and others, not just photocopy. It is a huge disappointment to say "I had that idea" or "that is exactly what I wanted to do," after seeing it elsewhere. Be the artist you want to see.

There are very few people who perceive the world in the same way. There are also very few people who can understand an alternate world in the same way. What you have is unique. Although great artists can be studied for practice, there is ultimately no need to be a complete copy of someone successful. We have already had enough of them. Focus on your own techniques as you learn about yourself and why you are so valuable.

After your first piece, or even after your first portfolio of pieces, do not stop there. Keep going. Always advance your work.

Challenge yourself with something bigger, or even more succinct. Learn from better artists and study more successful people. Try to be so good these great people want to work with you. Market and sell your work. Share your work and turn yourself into a business that can continue to grow and thrive for ages.

There is more to watch out for as you become successful and work with creatives more talented than you. You will find people who do not like what you do or always have something negative to say. Be prepared to either ignore these people or remove them from your life. Understand that not everyone has the same taste or view on life.

Some people have no perspective on life or a very negative view on life. Your art can help them, or maybe someone else's art can help them. But do not let them negatively affect you. More importantly, you will continue to gain feedback from those who dislike your work the most. This is valuable to grow as some people may not always provide you with the best constructive criticism.

As an unselfish artist, you find value in the work you do, and you see how you are helping others. Give back to those in the art community. Help others find their voice just as you found yours.

To become unselfish means, you have reached a point in your life where you can take care of your own needs and can help others.

Do not neglect to care for yourself, but understand that there is more to your life than you think. If you cannot give back to the arts community financially, donate time, or just take comfort in the idea that your works could provide visually appealing value to someone's life down the road. You need to find that person.

You have an opportunity to use your artistic voice for good. Not everyone is as fortunate as you to pursue a creative craft. Whether it is your work, time, or knowledge, do not forget to share, market, and sell. By doing so, you can provide for yourself, give back to society, friends, and family. By creating art, you become emotionally, spiritually, mentally, and physically fulfilled. Help others do this as well.

4. Increase Your Network

"In a writers' room...five brains are always better than one."
— Marian Yesufu, Comedy Personality

One of the most important and valuable skills in life is the ability to network. Capacity to find resources. Ability to connect with others who have similar and different opinions. Capacity to share and take in various life stories. The ability to connect with others and collaborate on bigger more impactful projects. Through better networking and connecting with a wider variety of people, opportunities to create greater art may become available. New networks help make new experiences and bring new knowledge.

If you are a quiet artist, this may be new to you, and that is ok. It might be scary to network outside of your own social circle. But if you can remove your fears you can create a much larger world. While not every artist aspires to lead and create movements, they do at least want to share a message. To socialize about art is human. To have valuable conversations regarding the arts is beautiful.

Take an opportunity to begin socializing whether that is online or off. Find your comfort zone, then as your art improves, start getting out of your comfort zone. Dive in and get out of your comfort zone. I did not let a minor fear of criticism keep me from writing and sharing my work.

Networking is a skill that continues to build your confidence, and you get better as you practice more. You begin even learning more about yourself and others as you ask questions and talk about yourself more. Innovative ideas are generated. Being social and developing networking skills can also lead to a better life.

It is fine if you prefer a very tight-knit circle of people, but eventually, you might want to network through them. Unless your five best friends are highly successful artists, you may want to find more people with similar interests. You never know what you can learn from meeting someone new. You might pleasantly uncover they appreciate your art.

Networking does not have to be intimidating. You might do it occasionally. You might ask your friend for another friends' number, or your parent for a cousin's new address to send them mail. You do not necessarily need to aim for the top people in an industry just yet. Trying to reach an incredibly successful film director may seem like a daunting task.

Just posting on a Facebook group for producers might be a great first step. You likely have wider network than you think. I know I am sometimes surprised when I speak with friends, and they mention they know someone very successful. With that said, you must eventually know what value you bring with the art you are unselfishly sharing with the world.

If for some reason, you are not comfortable connecting with difficult to reach, busy executives, and you are not comfortable going through family or friends, you can try random people online. There are hundreds if not thousands of websites and interest groups you can access to discuss your art with others. These may be conversations with people just like yourself who are more comfortable networking online as well. Find a way to meet them in person if possible.

As an artist, you will not necessarily network just to connect with new people, but also so they can help you hone your message. By having conversations about their work and your work, you can get the valuable feedback you may not be able to provide to yourself.

As you begin working on your art, it is valuable to have expert input. Not every expert will agree with your views or share their secrets, but you can get their opinion. Focus on questions and learning, then you will eventually build greater conversational skills. Think about the value other people can bring to your life and appreciate them for that.

You must be prepared, however, to accept feedback you do not agree with. Build that skill, and you can become much more successful. Fail to realize your flaws, and you may become stuck or disillusioned.

By listening to criticism, you can demonstrate humility. Self-criticism is not always honest because it is not necessarily how the world may see you. Your network can help you in many ways to include: overcoming minor obstacles, helping you where you are weak, or at least helping you find others who are willing to help you succeed. Learn about others and their struggles, and relate to a variety of people. You can create greater more meaningful art this way. Your view of the world is unique, and by listening to others, you also make your own story more connected and engaging. Learn and work to become an expert yourself. By accepting help, you can learn how to help others better as well.

After you develop your skills further, you have an opportunity to start teaching others. You may not master or become an expert or guru on your art, but there is something you know that someone out in the world does not. Whether it is your technique or a way you do your art that cannot be easily described yet, you have valuable knowledge to share. Try applying knowledge unrelated to your art, to someone else's work.

Many successful people have biographies written about them that are very helpful to others. Share your thoughts and find out who can relate to what you are saying. There are cookbooks created by famous chefs, classes taught by successful business executives, and case studies created from the greatest business or science projects. Build your self-confidence, enhance your art, and increase your own network.

As you begin receiving and giving help, you gain recognition as more of an expert. However, you must continue building on what you are learning. Improve not only your art but your skills as well. Everything is to make you a more successful artist that stands above the rest. You can take opportunities to connect other ideas with what you now work with. When you create new articles, songs, trinkets, websites, comics, or more, you can credit or reference the experts you have met to have more credibility.

A larger network also means bigger responsibility for leadership. People will want to associate with great artists. Your tastes may change. It is important to know the causes you stand for. These could include: diversity, animal rights, poverty alleviation and more. This will help you focus in on what events to go to or what groups to join. You can seek out even deeper underlying issues to speak for.

Most of what you hear on the news is very surface level. Learn to dive deeper by becoming more involved, networked, and educated on the subjects you care about. Your art may even spread a valuable message you are not aware of yet because of your own interpretation. It is great to truly work with the people you are speaking out for, or with.

Networking helps grow your resources to create more art tremendously. Watch the credits for your favorite film which can include hundreds of names. Nothing great is done alone. Great hermit artists of history were made great by those who found their art and shared them in galleries throughout the world.

You must cultivate your network. By doing so, you can help yourself, and others have access to greater projects. Not only is this for finding opportunities to develop your craft, but it is also an opportunity to find greater diversity in others' thoughts and opinions to combine into a masterpiece.

As you gain comfort in reaching into your network, you can uncover ways to share your art. One person may be an expert in marketing, another person might have expertise on YouTube, and another may know how to raise money to manufacture your new invention. Learn about what those in your network need help with, or what they enjoy, and you can bring constant value. Whether you are starting a business or taking your art to create a business, networking is necessary for development. The more opportunities you have, the more your art can grow.

Aim to improve increasingly so you can develop the confidence to go big. Your network can help you make bigger bets. I am not talking about gambling. I am talking about taking more calculated chances or pursuing more ambitious work. This will also make a better story for yourself when you succeed.

Do not be afraid to mess up. You can restart and take in lessons from earlier mistakes to do even better. Mistakes happen. Look at all the internet blog publications we trust for our news and see how often they include corrections. Work hard, go bigger, and share your story as an artist.

With social media, today, you are just a few clicks away from the world's most successful artists. You will not reach them without showing them how you can improve the world, or a powerful message, but the opportunity is there. They also become easier to reach as you build your influence by creating wonderful art, helping others, and gaining credibility. Do not be scared to take others advice and continue your networking whenever you can.

At some point, if you master networking, it is possible to lose focus on your art. You may realize you want to become a socialite, and that is ok if that becomes your art. Keep making more art and do not just focus on opportunities to make money (which will come) but also find ways to build confidence, valuable relationships, and ways to bring more value to the world. You can then connect with others who value your art as well which is fulfilling as well.

Do not forget that when you become successful, you will gain both people who dislike and adore your work. Do not let it dissuade you from your craft.

5. Impact the World

"As an artist, my work is meant to be seen. My art is meant to influence people and affect them. If I don't get it into the public, it has no purpose other than to enhance my life as a hobby, which is selfish."

— Kathleen Roy MFA, Actress and Educator

Take a moment to think of your favorite artists. What are they known for? What era did they live in? What were the changes happening that made them create what they did? What hidden meanings did the artist have in their works? What drove them to make their art?

Artists can improve the world. Consider for a second all the challenges you had growing up or issues you faced. Then think about a list of all the issues affecting the entire world. Dig down into the challenges, and put yourself in others' shoes.

Your art may not resonate with a global message yet, but a single photo in a popular magazine from a third world country can send ripples across the world. Incorporate the messages you believe are important into your works. They do not always have to be completely obvious. They can be subtle or symbolic. Maybe they do not even exist, except in over-analysis by fans in the future, and that is ok too.

Consider creating works bigger than oneself. The world stagnates without great creatives and scholars. If you never try to advance or share your work, one day you may find yourself wanting even more fulfillment. Start early and choose a cause to work with. Drive social change. Do not underestimate your ability to improve your own life and others lives.

Art is powerful. Use it to support those in need or create messages to help the defenseless. Find ways to save the planet through your work. Some famous actors are very well known for pushing for helping Polar Bears survive as our ice caps begin to melt. Show others that even if they are not doctors, or need to reset their lives, they can use art to spread important messages. It does not have to be through decades of research experience necessarily. A message can come from a dream.

Opportunities for social change can come from non-profit organizations. You may not necessarily make art for a non-profit, but you can make art, join organizations that support the arts, and become a success and volunteer your time or name. Give back to the community. Continue honing your messages as you become more attuned with what challenges others are facing or what issues non-profits have when trying to make a change. You can be entrepreneurial and sell your art to give back to those important causes.

Every event you go to can help you broaden your scope of experience and network. Continue seeking out those leaders in your community when you are focusing in on your cause. Do not wait to start, or let fear hold you back. Start creating art, or experimenting. One project will lead to another, then another, then another.

Community leaders may hear you out if you have enough conviction or truly have a thought-provoking piece of work. Even if your work does not seem "brilliant," it can appeal to someone if you search hard enough to get the message to them. But to know who that person is, you must network.

Major change: social movements, acceptance, poverty relief, and saving the planet all require change leadership. Individuals who take charge. Leaders. Find your strengths as a leader and artist, and focus on those to continue driving change. Maybe you are completely terrified of any marketing or sales. If you can come out of your fear, you can then help others.

Start with knowing what you can do. Anyone can create some art at this very moment whether it ends up in a fancy museum or not. Listen to what people want, and seek to either deliver or use their feedback to make more.

Begin considering how you can team up with others to create a message. An invention to remove toxic waste from the ocean requires a team. Learn how to collaborate. As you meet new people who share your vision, your work can spread much quicker. Furthermore, you can share responsibility and have someone help hold you accountable. You are not looking for a babysitter; you are finding a teammate.

Try and take these great peers, teammates, and leaders you meet and create small groups or tribes with them. Develop the soft skills necessary to work with a variety of people and significantly improve your work. Having multiple visions can often be better than just one and be ready to adapt to someone else's.

Do not be selfish by keeping your art to yourself, but also, do not be selfish by thinking your art is the only way to create. Through groups or tribes as some people like to call them, you can double or triple (or more) your focus as everyone around you becomes like a laser beam. Find people you can hold accountable and who hold you accountable. Keep up with the latest news and events that impact your group and continue growing our work and network.

By working for a meaningful social change, you can build trust with others who are affected. Trust takes long to build so do not start too late. Or it requires complete, intense focus and dedication. Without trust and integrity, your organization or business will fail in the long run, and you will not have long-term success.

People have a great intuition to know who you truly are. You must truly believe in what you are doing. This is usually easy when you are working on a great project, but for other initiatives where you may not be all in, believing in yourself is critical to success. But you should not be doing something you do not actually believe. However, this does not mean "do nothing" until you truly believe in it. Things are not always better on the other side and maybe sticking with where you currently are is the best option.

If you decide to pursue the route of creating art that creates good social change, you have an opportunity to hone in on your values and morals. You create better alignment and focus in your life. If you did not create art with some goal of a social change, that is ok too.

Perhaps you just want to capture and record beauty, or ugliness. There is a social change message there to appreciate both beauty and ugliness. You do not have to become the CEO of an organization that wants to alleviate world hunger, but you can take a stance and find ways to affect the movement through art. Use social change to guide your art and stick to your word.

It might be easier said than done to create or be a part of a movement. It does not necessarily have to be humanitarian either. What if you just want people to adopt a new way of pursuing their lives or art? The ideas in this book are just ways to enhance your art. Including symbols in your art is a way for people to examine and study your work. Not everyone will take time to study your entire portfolio, but you have a chance to leave clues and enhance your work.

Try to include meaningful messages that might require a second take, although many of these may occur unexpectedly through more experience just as comedians may unconsciously say something funny more often than a rocket scientist. Consider changing the way someone believes the world works. Emotion and art have more power than logic alone.

Social change can help increase the value of your art. If you are a writer, people enjoy connecting with others who are in the know about certain topics. If you share a valuable idea with someone who never thought of that, you will seem smart, and they will feel smarter too.

Value is also in the eye of the beholder. If presented with a choice, would you rather buy something that contributes to a better world, or something with no meaningful message at all? As society changes, your art can bring more value to the world as well. You can transform your works as time goes on, and you may even need a course correction in your approach or message, but it all begins by starting.

As an artist, you can capture the world as you see it. You can capture how you believe others view the world. You can make jokes or beauty from every day events. You can make people in the future question the present. Do not fear capturing the good or the bad of society as both can teach valuable philosophical lessons.

How do we know what people looked like over one thousand years ago? It is through the preservation of clothes, paintings, and writing that are all aspects of art. Try to capture a piece of history through your own life. Maybe help others share their story.

Keep the focus on your art until you become completely bored due to success, or need a dire change for whatever reason. Changing course is ok. Time moves fast today, and adaptability is critical. Take a message right away as a guiding force. It is not easy to find your guiding force right away. For example, if you believe in education, volunteer at the library. If you want to cut pollution, do a beach clean-up. As you do those activities, remember to network, and find learning opportunities, while also sharing your own story. Get small wins as you continue against bigger obstacles. Remember a win does not necessarily have to be a trophy. Getting feedback from a group of people can be just as valuable if not more valuable than a couple of dollars.

What can happen if there is no greater good you are working towards? The follow-up question is, what happens when you lose motivation? At least if you can focus on a greater good, you realize you are working towards helpful, as opposed to "uncertainty." The surer you are that a cause you are working towards is valuable, the more likely you will stay motivated towards it. You may take a break, a sabbatical, a nap, but eventually, you can get back on the path, or even change paths.

Having a social change in mind gives you an opportunity to make decisions easier because you know where to focus. Do not be scared to reinvent, rebrand, and try something new that might work better for you, but you must do something.

Take a step towards making your art today. Before moving onto the next chapter, write down a list of three social issues that might keep you or someone you care about up at night. Start thinking about how you can support social change initiatives through art. Let's say you want to make an eco-friendlier world – you can start doing doodles of trees. Get started.

***

***

6. Opportunity in Social Media

"Marketing is all about creativity. There isn't a wrong way, but there isn't a right way either. Finding a way to separate yourself from others is what marketing is about."

- AJ Tjaden, Marketing Influencer

We are in the greatest time in history for artists, creatives, inventors, tinkerers, and entrepreneurs. There are banks with billions of dollars and uncertainty with how to use it. There are millions of questions and problems to solve. There are desires and needs that require fulfillment. Opportunities to create change, sell art, and build businesses are abundant. Of course, they are easier said than done.

This book is not about telling you "how to" find every resource for success as an artist. This book is to show you that you can be great with your art. This book is to tell you about the basics and how you can dive into a new or current art with fervor.

Social media has billions of users throughout dozens of major platforms, all for various purposes. Artists have more visibility than ever before. After the first town meetings, the telegraph, the radio, telephones, television, and dial-up modems, we have abundant opportunities in social media.

While learning all the techniques and science to master social media, know that different platforms use different techniques to find the most relevant content for its' users. Start a profile as you begin creating art is the first step. Do not just pick one platform, but explore the others and try to dive into different social channels that may interest you. You may find your content or strategy resonates more with one or the other.

Many successful businesses can come from social media, just as most of the world's successful companies use social media as a login. There are easy to set up selling tools for your art whether you have one piece or many. You can now set up a shop by putting one of your artworks on an e-commerce platform then market through social media. If you prefer to share more work in written mediums, you can monetize blogs or find deals to monetize. Your art is your product, and there are many ways to monetize.

On the one hand, you can learn every aspect of doing business online yourself, there are plenty of free and paid resources to speed up your education. Overall, the tools you need are all in just a handful of places. By handful, I mean their apps can fit onto a single page in your mobile phone all with simple to use logins and more.

As you hone your art, you can simply post a picture and begin doing business. It may take a while, and it may not be easy once you start, but as you pick things up, you will develop your skills further.

We focused a lot on networking, and doing so in person is a must, but fortunately, the internet provides greater opportunities for those who do not have that luxury for whatever reason. Perhaps you live in a small town of just a few thousand people where nobody appreciates purple-colored flip flops.

Fortunately, you can find groups online of not only people who may buy your product, but also people who may want to sell your product for you, or who can help you improve your idea. Join forums, social media groups, professional organizations online, and as you gain more traction, you may even get invited to private secret groups. Get involved. The opportunity is greater than ever.

We touched on the subject of criticism as a learning experience. Do not let negative opinions hurt you. Let them be a growth and development opportunity. Unfortunately, people on the internet can be very negative. Fortunately, there is an even larger population on the web who can support your art.

You may be familiar with social media, but when you start sharing your art more, you will become more acquainted with others' opinions. Know that there will be great support and terrible reviews. Of course, you will want to team up with those who believe in you or want to help. Do not be afraid if you have to find someone to help bring your product to market, but beware – make sure the people you work with are worth working with. Do your research.

You may hear people tell you that you will not succeed because the time has passed. Sure, the easy opportunities to share and sell your art may have passed, and there may be opportunities coming up for "an easy win" in the future. But our mission is to create valuable art, and share it. To not be selfish against ourselves and keep our dreams locked up.

Create or build, snap a photo, upload it, and keep moving. You do not want to wait three years for the next big thing only to think back and say, "I should have started three years ago." You may waste some time, but learn from it, and try again.

I had my own blog where I wrote hundreds of posts, short stories, and articles, but shut it down because it was not where I wanted it to be and started over. Businesses run out of money then get bought out and gain new life. It is ok not to succeed at first, but it is not okay to not try.

Do not let others' success intimidate you. If everyone stopped trying only because the most successful person in their industry had it all, then we would never have new art. Innovation and change would die along with every dreamer, thinker, and doer.

Begin building your modern soft skills through social media. While face to face, in person interactions will always have power, there is still art and value to driving massive conversations on social media platforms. There are plenty of opportunities to just be the introvert you are on social media while still promoting yourself and developing your work.

Train yourself slowly as you gain more confidence talking to others. You will find many people have overcome greater challenges than yours. Practice regular writing and copywriting. Learn about others, make friends, and build more major social circles throughout the various social media platforms. Communicate, interact, share your opinions, and more. The digital soft skills will continue to gain prevalence and so will selling your projects and marketing.

It can be overwhelming understanding every platform, but fortunately, people will move towards those most helpful to them in large numbers. Find the ones that regularly pop up or are discussed on social media or that have huge numbers of users. Even smaller numbers of users from specific niches can help you.

If you seek a more business-oriented art such as writing sales copy, you could benefit from a business-oriented social network to connect with executives and managers. You can seek and read more about the news impacting the world on these platforms if you are the intellectual type and had enough pet videos for the day.

While I would promote being a part of major business networks, perhaps this is not for you. Maybe you want to solely focus on art and let other people handle your business. That is fine too. There are massive platforms dedicated to interpersonal social networks and fun entertainment.

Find a social media tool for artists by exploring them all, then find which one has the most users with similar interests. I do not list any specific platforms because although there are the top platforms with more users, this might prevent you from uncovering a platform perfect for you.

While some platforms are better for general sharing about your life, and others better for photographers or models, there are other platforms for filmmakers, speakers, and internet personalities. You can leverage more than one platform.

If you prefer to make videos, find an exciting video platform and connect with those users. You can even connect different video platforms with the general platforms that can reach an even larger audience. Many great artists have become successful sharing their works on these digital platforms.

As you continue exploring the social media channels, you will notice that the successful influencers with the largest followers work throughout all the different platforms. Their names will pop up all over because they are not selfish with their work. They are finding as many opportunities as possible to share their work with the world. It may be of benefit to you to also try new ones occasionally.

Platforms are known to go in and out of fashion. While some may be around longer than others, it is important to spread your art throughout. Nothing wrong with sharing your art in five places. Painters may present their work in multiple galleries. Through social media, you can share your art even quicker to a larger audience. Most of all, continue finding a platform that works best for you. Experiment.

As you begin using social media more, you will interact, and people will interact with you. Take in their considerations. Also, consider what people are trying to say. What their needs or desires are, and create your art to help them. Visit relevant art groups or pages and see what people are talking about. Watch videos and try to study what makes them entertaining. Begin to find other artists like you and see if they can teach you a lesson or give you a tip or two.

One thing you will get bombarded by on social media is advertisements. This is how these companies bring so much social value to you without you having to pay to join the platform. Eventually, you will want to sell your art and realize advertisements can help until you have greater recognition.

Advertising is an art itself; there is no need to put down other artists making a living. Consider learning from the ads, testing out your own to sell your art, and getting rid of ads you believe are irrelevant. The computer scientists have designed ads so that you find the products most relevant to help you. Sure, they want your money and attention, but if you learn to ignore or remove wasteful ads from your newsfeeds, you can focus even more on your craft.

Social media scientists have a benefit of helping you find the most relevant and valuable product for your success or life. You might even find a great deal on painting supplies for your next project. Ads are not an enemy, although they can be a nuisance if companies go overboard.

When you share your art, you will find ways to track your progress through analytics and tools that come with the platform. You can see where fans are watching from, when they stop watching your videos, and even how people are engaging with you.

Let this help guide what you need to do to improve. People will tell you whether they like or dislike your video. Figure out ways to get more eyes on it. You will need to learn to manage your time to learn all the various aspects of being an artist in today's digital world.

You can also find others to handle the digital issues for you. Either way, do not miss an opportunity to engage on social media and figure out what works or does not work. Something as simple as including a hashtag in front of a keyword for your art can get hundreds of views or more.

Start today. Before the next chapter, write down the social media platforms you now use. Then do a search, and write down five platforms you have not used or have not heard of. Next to each of those platforms, both ones you use and have not used, write ways you can use them for an art you want to pursue.

Ideas include taking photos of art and posting them, sharing a page of your book, and interacting with others about their art. Take action whether that involves starting a new profile, creating a new page for your art, or simply taking a step to improve your profile. See you online.

7. Plan Your Artistic Future

"People have to learn and understand all the skills in the industry. We would all have more work if everyone created, instead of just waiting for other people to hand them gigs."

— Kyle Wigginton, Actor and Filmmaker

You have a reason for creating art, you have your network of friends, and maybe you already even have a small portfolio. Take some time to plan for the future. Consider what happens when your art improves. Think about opportunities to sell your work. Consider what education or learning opportunities you might want to pursue. Think about what you need to broaden your work.

Depending on your art, consider creating an outline for your work. Cartoonists and painters start with outlines and guides on paper of how their vision will appear on paper. If you have an activity such as writing a book, or creating a business, take a moment to come up with an outline. Define your art, and write steps as to how you can promote your work, and what a sale might look like down the road. Start to gather your concepts and ideas into a single document. This will help initially, and you can continue developing and honing your plan as an artist as you go.

You do not need a business plan to become a painter, but if you want to use your painting skills to build a business for let's say, painting murals, you will need to have at least an idea of how you plan to accomplish that. Accept that you may not be able to do everything and figure out your strengths.

Today, artists must be versatile. You cannot just be a painter or singer. The greatest entertainers today are all businesspeople too. I challenge you to find one top performer in the world who is only a singer and does not dance or act, or invest, or speak live, or represent fashion brands. Those activities all need plans. You must come up with your outline until you become successful enough that you can hire smart people to do it for you. Begin setting yourself up for success in the future.

If you have not decided on an art to try yet, choose right now. If it is a screenplay which requires a team of people, you likely will not create it right now, but you can at least start drawing out a scene, or a title, or logline, or think of a good way to frame a shot. Evaluate what you know to do a project. Figure out what art, or aspect of a larger masterpiece you can accomplish now. Take this step also to understand the underlying message you want to present, and who your work might appeal to. Create art for others. Find a muse if you must.

This chapter is about preparing you for the intimidating aspects most artists might not be ready for. This includes selling, marketing, and networking which can all lead to fear and criticism. Think about the platforms you can sell and market your work. If you are a guitarist, think about ways to join a band, make videos of you playing guitar, or find venues to play in. You should be ready to dive in. Draw your first line, pluck your first string, write your first sentence, and do not be scared to share it with your friends, family, and strangers.

Begin asking yourself questions such as "who would buy my art? What is the worst thing someone could say? Does my artwork suit this social media platform? How else can I add to my credibility as an artist?" Assume the world, or at least someone is waiting for your work. Write down the answers you come up with.

It is ok to create and find out it does not interest you somewhere down the road. Therefore, you must at least try now and find out as soon as possible whether you are truly passionate about your craft or not. Even if you get bored after a month, you can return to it somewhere down the line.

Consider setting your hobby up to be a potential career opportunity. But do not wait to find out you do not enjoy it. Do a long-term outline, an end goal, but some attainable short-term milestones. You cannot end world hunger with a billion, or even a million dollars, what makes you think you can stop it by doing absolutely nothing? While it may seem daunting, one step can have a ripple effect or at least help.

Depending on the complexity of your goals, you may be able to create a small portfolio of work right now. Want to be a poet? Start a collection of twelve haikus. Your haikus could inspire a video in the future, or even a writing business. If your work is complicated, such as inventing a plane that can run entirely on electricity, you at least need to draw out what a plane now looks like, and a few sketch concepts of how it could work, and an outline of companies that may invest in your projects.

Mostly everything can start with a pen and paper, from the simplest sketch to the most complex mathematic algorithm. You can even try to pull up something someone else has accomplished and just build off of that for practice.

If you are still afraid to get started with making art, perhaps get friendly advice. Ask a friend if you can draw something for them, or if they need any help with ideas. Your art could be consulting. Chances are, you are not so much afraid to create art.

Anyone can draw a doodle then burn it never to be seen by the world. But to build a career from your work, and to help the world takes altruism. Again, you do not have to save the world. The social cause is to guide your art, and prepare it so that someone may one day find value in what you are doing.

When planning, try to map out your network. This is a bit more easily done with social media because you can find out how people are connected and the degrees of separation from you. Consider maps to reach out to galleries or invention buyers. More than mapping out potential buyers or fans of your art, keep up to date with the current friends who may help.

The major catch-22 in many aspects of our lives is you must have, to do more. You must have experience to get experience, or you must have work to get work. It is annoying, but no matter how small your first step is, have some art, so that people can view you as an artist. If you are not ready to be considered as an artist yet, start building your portfolio, and plan how you can position yourself as an artist.

Somewhere along the path, you will need to take a risk. This may be financial such as investing in an educational course, buying a high-priced easel, paying to market your work, or even the mental risk you take when you share content only to become depressed because no one "likes" it. Take a chance to feel uncomfortable. Sometimes creating is the easy part, but sharing it is much harder.

Take a risk with your message. I am not saying just to start spouting off offensive babble. I mean take a chance, do something a little edgy, and do not be afraid to create a meaningful, honest conversation on an important topic. Do not limit yourself with usual social conventions of being overly polite. That does not help the artist.

As you create art, think of ways to challenge yourself, and you can learn how others can challenge you. Address those ahead of time. Challenge yourself by both creating limitations and removing them. This sounds contradictory, but take a filmmaker for example. Challenging a filmmaker to create a film based on a single premise can offer just as much of a challenge as telling them to come up with something from nothing (although that can be a premise in itself – a story about writer's block).

Let your work debate social injustices, support social good, or even depict the struggles you have in your daily life. Change the way you think to become a better artist. I cannot cover all the separate ways to change your thinking, but if you search, you will find.

At this point, you should have at least had a doodle, or an idea, or a sentence written about an art you wish to pursue. Start bringing together more resources even if you must spend money. Do not procrastinate. The more time you spend doing, the closer you get to mastery.

By spending money on your art, you become more invested. It becomes more than just an "attempt" at a craft. Do not just throw money at something expensive at first. Start small. Find ways to do things for free at first until you develop a better system or become more successful.

Set a goal for your next project. Do not just set an ambiguous goal, but learn to set a goal that can be accomplished. Let us take making a movie for example. You may not have the skills or resources right away to make an award-winning feature film. But you will need to develop certain skills that you may not have right now.

Your goal must thus, be attainable. You can create an award-winning feature film in a few years, but first, you need to learn the art itself. Make a goal to produce a short film within the next six months, then halve that time. Pick a minor or major action that takes you closer to that goal, set a date to do it by, then execute on that action.

Depending on how you learn, all this design, planning, and writing or drawing can help in other ways. Some people learn better visually. Studies show most people learn more when physically writing information. Others may learn better by sound.

Everyone can learn better by regular practice, repetition, and improvement. Keep your plans handy and be ready to adjust them as the times change.

It is important to carry out these tasks simply because, as an artist, you must be able to set your schedule. Bosses do not bind an artist, but artists must responsibly use their freedom to succeed. Seek inspiration, find customers, and seek guidance, but do not be waiting for someone to tell you exactly what and how to carry out a task.

Start building these good habits for the future when you can look back and say, "I am glad I did not wait around for my art to just succeed by itself." Set aside time to work and plan for success.

As you build your portfolio, keep track of everything. Check in on your progress towards your goals. Find ways to categorize different projects. Keep track of the amount of time you dedicated to each and see where you got stuck.

Certain arts do not need extensive analysis from the artist because what was created is done, and that is that. Other arts and a career in arts requires regular evaluation. Evaluate what fans are saying, what methods you need improvement on, or what you failed to accomplish in your previous works. Check back with your plan and see if it needs adjustment.

Keep up with practicing. Draw, write, play, share, tinker, sculpt, or do every day. Seek to improve your work until you have mastered it. Plan to have a bigger impact than you believe you are capable of. Get started, practice, and do not stop pursuing your art. Taking a break does not necessarily mean you have "stopped." It just means you needed to refresh. Feel free to share your art with me on social media.

8. Share Your Value

"I want to use my artistry and my love for science to make science fun and available to everyone. A lot of people are scared of the sciences, but when you start pairing fun facts with cute little creatures, it makes the information more digestible and may change the way some see the world."

– April Kissinger, Scientist and Creator of Miscreation Nation Creatures

Marketing is sharing how you bring value to the world. It is about getting yourself out there and letting people know what you are capable of. You have incredible value, and it is a shame if no one ever knows about it. Market how your art helps others, what type of message you are trying to send, and how others can join to help. Everything up to this point in the book is to prepare you to have a project to market. Even if you have only drawn a line, you can build a story off that as your art improves.

Start marketing and prepare to turn your art into a business. Grow your art, grow your brand, increase your success, and learn to live off your work. Develop your digital and soft skills so you can build a business. The opportunities are there. You want to be an artist, you want to create art, but you must also learn the other aspects required to succeed as well. If you are starting from absolute nothing, the things already mentioned are tasks you must accomplish. Thrive and help more people.

Does your art make a strong social statement? Does your art make people think about an injustice? Does your art make people think or want to take action or change their perspective in some way? Your voice fits somewhere into the world and can help you figure out what message you want. It may change as you go, but have it for now as you create.

As you begin learning about ways to market your art, you build skills that you can use for a long time. Marketing has been around for a very long time. It is one of the most valuable skills in the world, so not only does your art benefit, but so do your own abilities. Learning new skills, studying free courses online, all of these can help you leverage extra time you may have. Enjoy this ability to build new skills constantly. You could find a new passion.

Have you ever heard of the person who made a movie that had no impact on anyone? Nope. Who is that person? Every success story knows marketing or has someone on their team that knows some form of marketing. Major social media successes today market themselves day in and day out, almost every hour of the day.

Great successful artists often have teams with them. Even the independent painters or sculptors have people they go to for paint, stone, or inspiration. Fear of marketing should not be an issue. Figuring out how may be a challenge, but try. People who matter will care about your projects. Keep them in mind and keep them in your tribe.

When you market, remember one key factor: that you create art for others, not yourself. Sure, there might be relaxation and a boost in confidence when people like your art, but ultimately, your art is for someone else. Do not worry about fame or fortune; those can come.

Making art is what matters. Invent, paint, record to make life better. Keep searching for the beauty you see and be sure to share it. If not beauty, share valuable information, or ideas that no one has shared yet.

As more people hear about your art and how great it is, be prepared to sell and let go of your work, or let others have a piece of your work. You want to sell your art. If you do not sell your art, someone else will fill the void. By giving your art away without any goal or increasing the value in some way is not doing yourself justice.

If you do not understand what marketing is exactly, take a second to look up some free courses online. There are many great resources you can uncover with a simple search. Tackle the aspects that seem most interesting to you, and practice the skills you most want to learn. There are even skills you can learn that can boost your art. The foundational definition is simple.

Do not overcomplicate it with everything the web has to offer. Learn piece by piece, and focus on your own branding. It takes time to hone a larger message. It is, however, important that you hone your own personalized message, and get started.

Have confidence in your ability both to create and to share. Gain confidence in your new skills and adaptability. Have faith in your art, and it will show. At some point, you will have the credibility to advise others as well.

Consider taking someone in to help mentor or train. There is a huge market for learning resources now. Teach people something you wish you learned. Be like a superhero. Take on new responsibilities, new abilities, new skills, and be super.

Let your creation of art help you become the best person you can be. It is an expression of you, how you view the world, and a way to both inspire and motivate others. When you market and share your art, you are not just trying to get people to see it so you can sell it to them. You are communicating. You are telling a potentially untold story.

There are so many actions you can take, right now. If you do not have social media, hop on it right now and start jumping in every group you can. If you do not like the idea of social media, go search for a database of art galleries and start calling out to see how you can have your art shared. Take photos of your art and start leaving traces in the street, so other people pick it up or pass by it. Find other artworks, and build off it. Maybe even go volunteer at an art gallery or help work for an artist to get started. Visit an art school and start talking about art.

Times are changing, and it is incredibly exciting for all artists to have opportunities. Technology, although intimidating to newcomers, is exciting. Technology is fresh and tends to help simplify your life.

Embrace the new marketing technologies on the internet for your work. These are also tools you likely have to learn to succeed in the future even if you do not plan on using them directly. While your soul craves, and depends on art, you will need to understand marketing in the future anyway. Adapt to the times.

Narrow down your niche, learn about them, and figure out why you are helpful to them. Let your art have a positive impact. If you want to help the homeless, let your art aid them by appealing to people who can afford to buy your art so that you can have an impact on homelessness.

Consider interviewing homeless people as your own art form, or collect art from the homeless. Find where humanitarians hang out and go there. What want, need, or desire does your art fill? Let it be personal to you, but create it for others, and know that even if it was made just to share your perspective, someone could benefit from it.

Begin finding people and ask for them to act, even if it is as simple as looking at your art. This can help prepare you to learn to sell. Ask someone to tell a friend about your art, or ask them if they can tell you someone who could benefit. If you are more conscious of your goals, you can begin to help guide the people using your art or just viewing it. For example, if you are a digital artist that creates beautiful infographics, have someone view an infographic, then guide them to another, and another, then another. As this happens, do not forget to credit others who inspired you.

Track your progress and begin tying all your marketing platforms together. Learn from what you are doing. Improve your art and your business and technical skills all at the same time. You must do this to be unselfish and share your art with the world.

Keep track of all the projects you are working on. If you are not on social media, then there is no excuse to not spend your sole focus on building out your marketing options outside of social media. This all depends on what kind of art you are pursuing, but there are marketing opportunities for all arts.

Always keep improving on your content, ability to find more viewers, or even every message you decide to deliver. Feel free to "mess up" because any mistake might feel brilliant when you look back on your work.

9. Monetize

"Keep in the habit of creating. You want to always be making something because that will grow into your next project."
– Bonnie Kathleen Ryan, Actress and Filmmaker

You spent hours coming up with inspiration for your masterpiece, months creating and editing it, and now you shared it with the world. Suddenly someone wants to buy. Time to let go of your art. Now selling may not always be this easy unless the person handling the marketing was a miracle worker. You may eventually need to work for a sale, which by the way, is not as bad of a word as people try to make it out to be.

Times are changing, and salespeople are gaining more respect today than they had twenty or more years ago. Systems and checks are in place to keep sellers in check if they want to stay in business for long. Bad practices are bad for business. Salespeople are trained to have more integrity today.

Let us remember that everyone in the world sells from the CEO to the cashier. A CEO might position their company to sell to stockholders while a clerk may sell a French fry. You may do it without knowing it every time you talk about your favorite show so that your friend watches it. Every post on social media is trying to sell a joke, an idea, a thought, a picture.

Selling is happening all around us and critical to success in life. We do not dive into "how to sell" here as there are many articles out there. Just know that at some point, as an artist, you must learn to market and sell yourself and your projects.

Sales are as much of an art form as anyone else. An actor takes on the physical role from a writer's imagination as another artist gracefully explains the meaning of their art. Sales require creativity and process, just as developing a business, painting, sculpting, or inventing requires certain steps. It takes practice just like any other skill. And most importantly, you must learn to sell so others can become fascinated by those things fascinating to you.

Just like marketing, sales is an incredibly sought-after skill and yields highly paid careers. Most hard skills can be taught quickly. But the soft skills required for sales need much more time. The skills can also be used in your regular everyday life as you talk about ideas. Fortunately, there are processes to learn how to sell and create art. Keep searching, and stay focused on your goals. Focus on your strength, but learn a little bit about the various arts.

Boost your communication skills like no other. It is possible to be a quiet artist who creates masterpieces but is never able to express the work in words. Perhaps you could write it down and have someone else present it for you, but your art is your art. Learn to speak with people and sell your projects.

Learn the art of selling and increase your power of persuasion as well. Use sales to measure your success as you improve your skill.

Use the skills you build by learning about skills to not just market, but overcommunicate what you can deliver. Are you inventing a workout machine that works every single muscle in the body? Learn the ability describe it when you do not have one available to sell. Let others know what you are doing via word.

Tell others about who you are, and what you plan to deliver to them even if they are not the direct recipient of your work.

Above completing an art piece, closing a deal is a great feeling. Selling your work or someone else's is a great feeling. Consider that you are working on your own terms. You are both an artist and an entrepreneur. You have fed yourself in about every sense of the word. You have won someone over to find the beauty in your work. It is an amazing thing. How do you feel when people agree with you? Now how would you feel when someone both agreed with you and paid you for it?

Sales make the world go around, and it is not to be ignored. You will not have money to continue pursuing your art until you make more money. You can do that in a regular job, or you can share your art.

Build your work into a business. Then use your art to create logos around it or create the most beautiful business in the world. Explain why your business is an art itself. Then you can use the art of writing to share the story with the world. See how much other people's works are going for, what their causes are, and motivate yourself to come up with a price. Trade services for money.

You can paint or sculpt a new piece for someone's home. Sell your work as inspiration or wisdom. There are numerous opportunities to monetize your work today even without face to face selling.

Sales help you measure success financially. While money should not be the end all be all pursuit here, it is important. Other measures of success are how many new people you are connecting with. Another can include how many people you can bring to your non-profit gala which could involve financial success for the organization and not you. As you make money, you could give back to others which is an amazing feeling in itself.

Everything in this book is geared towards motivating you to create and helping you build other skills around your art that are useful. Share your skills as a service. Simply by pursuing your art, you have developed skills to bring more value to the world. Build those skills so you can make even more use of your time. Do not forget to find ways to let others balance out your weaknesses too if you need to.

Many online tools make selling as simple as snapping a photo, uploading it, then waiting for a notice that you must deliver. Sometimes you can even skip having to deliver yourself. Social media makes it incredibly easy to advertise, and some technologies make advertising even more targeted.

You must eat to survive, and thus you must learn these skills to be unselfish and share your art. These skills are to help you survive (spiritually, financially, and more) and thrive. Creating art is a survival skill as it fuels your soul. Marketing, sales, networking, and creating social change are all necessary to help you navigate life and make a better world for others to live in.

If you do not begin to take on some of these other skills, you can fall very behind on technology. Some people will share their art and compete with you against your will unless you learn how to do these things. You do not need to master everything, but you do need to understand what it takes to be a successful known artist today.

The world is changing quickly with every new app and phone upgrade. Brands go in and out of style quicker than ever before with new brands entering the market and old brands leaving. Branding is an art form. Understand you must keep adapting.

Handle your art, create something, and upload it today. Set up an e-commerce website that allows you to sell relatively easily.

There are many to choose from and even ones dedicated to specific types of craftspeople and artists. Create your social media profiles and connect with old friends. Start uploading your work to both pages and network, market, sell.

10. Fearlessly Pursue Your Work

"Never fear judgment – learn to appreciate the unique qualities that make you special and run with them! As long as you have a positive faith in your personal character, there is no 'risk' involved in 'putting yourself out there.' As strong sense of self will deter you from falling victim to unhealthy criticisms from unhappy people. It's your life. Live it for YOU!"

- Bridgette Meredith Garb, Model and Actress

The best thing you can do for yourself is to take a dive and jump in even though the water is cold. You will warm up as you start doing. Do not sit and wait for inspiration to come. The more you do, the more inspiration will come and eventually you will have so much inspiration your problem becomes deciding which projects to do.

Pick up a pen, get a notebook, or pick up a phone. Draw, edit, design, map, sketch, breakdown, photograph, sing, dance, act, etc. Whatever it is you want your art to be, do something right now no matter how minor.

Then take your next step, and then take an even bigger step. Evaluate where your work is now. Take a moment to break down your work and analyze what you carried out. Then consider how you can improve the next project, and how you can take an even bigger step than usual.

Try or do, but do not be idle. If you at least even try, you are doing. Stand up, roll over, pick your head up, and do. Put the book down if you must. Or say you will put the book down in the next thirty seconds, this way you have time to do it.

Enjoy yourself. Rub paint on your face. Smash the drums with your hands. Draw stick figures on a wall in an erasable way. Have fun with the creative process. Let yourself face challenges then overcome them as a champion. Most of all, overcome these pointless internal struggles or lack of confidence that have no reason to be there.

Explore a variety of arts. Try painting, then try writing a poem about the painting, then test out the art of selling your painting. There are infinite combinations of artistic endeavors that can start with a simple pen and paper. Do not just explore and do art, but learn about the history of your art, the biographies, and the modern techniques.

Keep the work coming. Do them quickly. You will know which works to take your time on, and which ones not to overthink. Do not let overthinking be the cause of your inaction. Let quality come as you learn. Quality is in the eye of the beholder, and although if we are honest, not everything is high quality, the world's greatest artists all have created unsuccessful work. Why be a one-hit wonder if you do not have to? Creating more quality products takes time.

The car as we know it today is not the same as the unairconditioned automobile of the past. Start developing, but first, you must set a foundation. Never stop learning how to get better.

Begin tracking every one of your projects. This will come in handy when people might want to know what else you have accomplished and this way you can tell them. Know where they are and evaluate why you may have sold one, stopped one, or why you enjoyed an artwork. Try not to repeat the mistakes that halted or hindered your artistic process. Remember what helped make you successful and reiterate that.

There are plenty of obstacles that could potentially halt your progress. Overcome them and come out on top. However, do not let it be a mental barrier. Every successful person had to find their mental obstacles that have no reason to be there, and eliminate them. Change your thinking to change your life and change the world.

So much of your art is mental. Was your mind in a good place or bad place when you started? Was it truly something you wanted to pursue or were you just infatuated with the idea of it? Remember that your art is unique, and combined with your story, it is multi-dimensional. No one else has your same voice and view of the world. Take what you learn and combine it with your current skills and you could create something never before seen.

As you make more art, you will find more opportunities to keep doing it. You will find ways to free up your schedule to do something you love. You will bring your friends and family in. Even when you get stuck, move onto a different project, then come back, and you can get unstuck. Help teach others when you are onto something new and exciting.

To accomplish all of this, if you have not done so already, consider creating a process. Either seek one out as I did with writing this book or create your own. A powerful system can help your projects thrive. That is how franchises are so successful throughout the entire world. That is how I wrote this book. Processes are usually harder to find since they may be secrets, but if you look long and hard enough, you will find it.

You owe it to everyone to get your art out in front of as many people as it takes until your work finds a home. Let other people appreciate your work, but do not fear the mainstream audience and what they might say about your work. Demonstrate service to others through the expression of your work. Help those helping you, but do not get worried about protecting your team by sticking to an inflexible routine. Not everyone knows how to find the beauty in ugly things. Keep sharing what your art is about, and even consider coming up with counter-arguments.

Share, share, share, and get out there! No matter how much work you have already completed, chances are you still have a masterpiece somewhere. Keep relentlessly putting your work in front of people. You need people. Start training in face to face communications and build good habits.

In the end, do not forget to deliver value. You already have a bunch of it stored up ready to give to the world. You must get your creations in front of others and available for sale. There is nothing wrong with having great attention to detail, but if you having nothing means no detail at all. Consider all the artistic endeavors that start out as thrown away drafts, resketches, and ideas on a napkin. You will have the opportunity to do wonderful things if you just let go of a fear of marketing or selling, and view it as something you do every single day regardless of if you have art or not.

Never forget the power of your artistic voice regardless of what that may be. Art is a wonderful way to leave your legacy with the world. To leave your mark, help others, inspire others, and shape the world.

About the Author

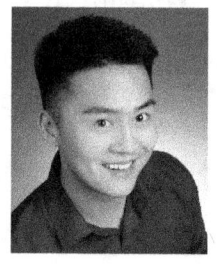 This is Emmett Ferguson's first published book, but not his first authorship. He has written stories, poems, business articles, and screenplays on his previous websites and social media. He also produces narrative content available on YouTube for your viewing pleasure.

He studies today's success stories and tests out ideas which he shares. He believes deeply in the practical advice of doing, taking steps, and not overthinking every action.

Your first step might make you highly successful, or maybe your first ten thousand steps might not work, but no matter what, nothing happens' without doing.

www.ingramcontent.com/pod-product-compliance
Lightning Source LLC
Chambersburg PA
CBHW071216240526
45470CB00018B/1874